HOW TO LEAD IN A WORLD

OF

DISTRACTION

MAXIMIZING YOUR INFLUENCE BY TURNING DOWN THE NOISE

STUDY GUIDE I SIX SESSIONS

CLAY SCROGGINS

ZONDERVAN
REFLECTIVE

ZONDERVAN

How to Lead in a World of Distraction Study Guide
Copyright © 2019 by Clay Scroggins

This title is also available as a Zondervan ebook. Visit www.zondervan.com/ebooks.

Requests for information should be addressed to:
Zondervan, 3900 Sparks Dr. SE, Grand Rapids, Michigan 49546.

ISBN 978-0-310-11516-8 (softcover)
ISBN 978-0-310-11517-5 (ebook)

Cover design: *Thinkpen Design*
Interior design: *Rob Williams, InsideOut Design*

First Printing November 2019 / Printed in the United States of America

CONTENTS

ABOUT
THE STUDY

I'm so easily distracted. I am guessing you are as well. None of us are immune to the growing cacophony of distractions around us. In the last few years, I've asked many people a simple question: *Are there more or fewer distractions in our world today than there were ten years ago?* The answer is always . . . wait, gimme a minute. Just need to check an email.

Okay. The answer is always a resounding, "More!" We all feel it. We are drowning in distractions everywhere we go. It's not just a problem in the workplace. It's an epidemic in our homes as well. I have too many stories of missing something in my kids' lives because my mind was consumed with something else. I actually have a story of missing *a kid* because of not being attentive in the present. Call it a "parenting fail."

My wife and I have five kids, and we were managing bath time for all of them. Our youngest, Whit, was finished with his bath and waiting on me to put on his diaper and pajamas. Evidently, he felt that he had waited long enough. I was distracted, fixing something on the camera in his room, and somehow I didn't notice him quietly crawling away.

It was only when my wife asked me to put Whit to bed that I realized . . . Whit was not there. He was not in the room. The gate on the stairs was open, so I headed downstairs to continue my search. Whit was not in the kitchen. Or in the living room. Or in the front hallway. That's when I saw the door leading outside was open. Whit was not in the *house*. I found him making his way down the street . . . completely naked. It was quite an amusing show for the four neighbors' houses that he passed.

We later laughed at the consequences of that distraction, but not all our distracted moments are so comical. Distractions take a toll on our marriages, our families, our friendships, our ability to think and manage tasks at work—and our ability to lead others. Distractions cost us in terms of opportunities we miss because we are not paying attention. Distractions pull us away from the important things in our lives. Distractions can keep us from living the best life that God has for us.

Distractions are often like white noise. They mask things we don't want to confront. In this study, we will look at how we can recognize these masking elements to uncover the feelings they are hiding. I believe we do this by adopting four practices:

- Finding simplicity
- Speaking to yourself
- Getting quiet
- Pressing pause

With these tools, you'll be empowered to replace the chaos in your busy world with an emotional competence that leads to a calmer, less stressful, and more fulfilling life.

Sound intriguing? Then I invite you to join me in this study. Together, we will discover how to turn down the white noise so we can lead ourselves and others—even in a world that is overrun with distractions.

HOW TO USE THIS GUIDE

GROUP SIZE

This study has been written with different groups in mind. Whether you're a leader at your organization or a stay-at-home parent, we believe the concepts will help you understand the problem of distractions, how to limit them, and how to adopt some practices to help your team deal with them and function more efficiently.

You can use this study in groups of all different sizes. But we think the ideal group size is eight to twelve adults or four to six married couples. Why? Because that's a large enough group to provide the diverse opinions that drive conversation, yet small enough that group members can hold one another accountable.

Accountability is absolutely crucial to the group dynamic. Reading this material, watching the videos, and having some discussions probably won't create a big, sustainable change in your personal life or in your leadership. That will only happen if you apply what you learn. And you'll probably succeed in application only if you have a group of people who are willing to encourage you and hold you accountable.

MATERIALS NEEDED

Here are the things you'll need for this study:

- This guide
- The accompanying teaching videos
- Something to write with
- A copy of the *How to Lead in a World of Distraction* book (optional for the group meetings but recommended for the between-sessions study)

That's it.

TIMING

The suggested time for each group session is 90 minutes. This can be broken down as follows:

Conversation Starter: *10 minutes*
The Conversation Starter is designed to tee up the session's topic while helping you to get to know one another a little better. This is especially helpful if your group is new.

Video Teaching: *15 minutes*
After the Conversation Starter, watch the session video teaching together. It will present the content that you'll discuss as a group.

Group Discussion: *45 minutes*

Spend most of the session having a conversation about the content you watched together. Use any of the Group Discussion questions to guide the conversation.

My Leadership Challenge: *15 minutes*

My Leadership Challenge provides a simple way to begin to apply what you're learning. Don't skip this section of the study. It will help you change and grow.

Session Wrap-Up: *5 minutes*

The Wrap-Up helps you to put a bow on the session, so to speak. It's an opportunity to reiterate the bottom line of the session's topic. It's also an opportunity to close the meeting in prayer, if you so choose.

Note that there are also suggested personal study activities for you to complete on your own in between the main group sessions.

FACILITATION

You probably have a mental picture of what it will look like to lead—what you'll say and how group members will respond. Before you get too far into planning, there are some things you should know about leading a group discussion.

Cultivate Discussion

It's easy to assume that a group meeting lives or dies on the quality of your ideas. That's not true. It's the ideas of everyone in the group that make a meeting successful. Your role is to create an environment in which people feel safe to share their thoughts. That's how relationships will grow and thrive among your group members.

Here's a basic truth about spiritual growth within the context of community: the study materials aren't as important as the relationships through which those materials take practical shape in the lives of the group members. The more meaningful the relationships, the more meaningful the study. The best materials in the world won't change lives in a sterile environment.

Point to the Material

A good host or hostess creates an environment where the people in the group can connect relationally. He or she knows when to help guests connect and when to stay out of the way when those connections are happening organically. As a group leader, sometimes you'll simply read a discussion question and invite everyone to respond. The conversation will take care of itself. Other times, you may need to encourage group members to share their ideas. Remember, some of the best insights will come from the people in your group. Go with the flow, but nudge the conversation in the right direction when necessary.

Depart from the Material

We've carefully designed this study for your group. We've written the materials and structured the questions to elicit the kinds of conversations we think will be most helpful to your group members. However, that doesn't mean you should stick rigidly to the materials. Knowing when to depart from them is more art than science, but no one knows more about your group than you do.

The stories, questions, and exercises are here to provide a framework for exploration. But different groups have different chemistries and different motivations. Sometimes the best way to start a discussion is to ask, "Does anyone have a personal insight you'd like to share from this week's material?" Then sit back and listen.

Stay on Track

This is the flip side to the previous point. There's an art to facilitating an engaging conversation. While you want to leave space for group members to think through the discussion, you also need to keep your objectives in mind. Make sure the discussion is contributing to the bottom line for the week. Don't let the discussion veer off into tangents. Interject politely in order to refocus the group.

Are you ready to begin? Then let's jump into the first session of *How to Lead in a World of Distraction*.

THE DANGER OF DISTRACTION

As someone said, you will never get to the end of your journey if you stop to shy a stone at every dog that barks.

WINSTON S. CHURCHILL,
FROM *CHURCHILL BY HIMSELF*

WELCOME

Welcome to *How to Lead in a World of Distraction*. I'm glad you've decided to take this journey. This study is about getting back on track in a world that will distract you right into the ditch.

You can certainly relate. Our society is perhaps the most stressed, depressed, and anxious group of humans ever to walk the planet—and that trend is accelerating. The types and frequency of the distractions have never been greater. The result? Shallow lives that lack focus, self-awareness, and passion. I'm not okay with this. I'm guessing you're not either.

My hope in this study is to set the stage for some group discussion that will help you realize the cost of these distractions in your life, understand what those distractions are masking, and then discover some simple practices for turning down the noise. This is essential, because before you can *lead others*, you first have to *lead yourself* by overcoming your own distractions. I've seen this transformation happen in countless lives, and I've experienced it on a personal level in my own life. I promise you—you can do it, and it is worth it.

When you first meet, do your best to let go of all distractions! Put aside your smartphones and be present in the moment with your group. Start by going around the room and introducing yourselves. Agree to be honest, engage fully, cheer each other on, and keep what's said confidential. You share a common desire to grow as leaders in this area. So commit to lean in and learn together!

SESSION OVERVIEW

None of us are immune to the distractions that are all around us. In fact, when CareerBuilder conducted a survey on distractions a few years ago, seventy-five of the 2,000 people surveyed said they lost two or more hours per day in productivity due primarily to smartphones, the internet, email, and social media. But the truth is we are losing so much more . . . and we need to recognize the toll that our distractions are taking on our lives.

You're the only one who can honestly judge your distractions, look at what they're costing you, and then do something about them. This is about learning to limit the distractions so you can gain traction on the path that reflects your true spiritual desires and be fully present to pursue the people and things that matter most. What could be more important than that?

CONVERSATION STARTER

Share a recent situation that went sideways because you were too distracted to be fully present. What were the consequences? How did you feel afterward?

VIDEO TEACHING

Watch the video segment for session one. A summary is provided for your benefit as well as space to take additional notes.

Summary

I imagine your life is filled with distractions. That's probably why you decided to go through this study. If you're anything like me, the chances you'll even get through this first session without being distracted are slim to none. Let's face it. **Distractions are real, distractions are significant, and distractions affect almost every area of our lives.**

I don't need to spend a lot of time telling you how distracted our world is. You already know that is true. There are more distractions today than ever before in the history of the world. Consider that we have a law that prohibits you from operating a motor vehicle while staring at your phone. That we even need this law is ludicrous—and it's a symptom of a deeper problem. It just stands to reason that if you're operating a machine of moving metal, you should probably focus on what's ahead. (I'm talking to myself at this point.)

Distractions know no age—this is not a generational thing, or a gender thing, or a temperament thing. I see distracted Baby Boomers. A good friend of mine called before Christmas and said, "My sixty-five-year-old parents are more distracted by their iPads than my five-year-old son. I honestly think I'm going to put restrictions on their devices!"

I see it in the Gen Xers. Not only is this generation of adults using their devices forty minutes more each day than their younger peers, but they are also the most likely to pull out their phones at the dinner table. Much of their device use is work related and commonly justified as necessary. That *need* to stay in touch with friends, keep up with the emails at work, and manage life can easily lead to habits of distraction.

Millennials are the generation that grew up with the internet. They are the we-don't-have-to-*not*-know generation. This awareness that somewhere out there the answer can be found has created an unprecedented level of distraction. Consider all the options we have now—Google it, or Shazam it, or Wikipedia it, or ask Alexa. We no longer have to *not* know.

Generation Z is distracted as well. Just walk onto any college campus and you will see every student staring at a screen. There is not enough ADHD medicine on the planet to allow me to focus in an environment where I have the internet, FaceTime, texting, or any other screen right in front of me and still try to listen to my economics professor. No chance.

But the greatest problem with distractions is that **none of us have a plan for handling them**. That is what this study is about: *how we can lead ourselves better in a world where the distractions are growing and growing.* But before we jump into that content, we first need to know why it's so important to have a plan for handling distractions.

There are three costs at stake. The first is the **opportunity cost of the unknown**. When economists and sociologists talk about opportunity costs, they are speaking of the benefits you miss out on by choosing one thing over another. What you don't know definitely *will* hurt you. What you don't know is what you're actually missing out on because of the opportunity cost of distraction. Every opportunity lost has a cost.

The second cost is a **lack of traction**. The word *distract* comes from the term *tract*, which is "to draw," and *dis*, which means "away from." So a distraction is something that draws you away from the traction you have. Traction is important. Just think of what it means when you're driving down the road. Traction compels you forward in life. If you're not careful, your distraction-filled days can lead to a traction-less life.

A third cost is the **failure to live your best life**. I think we're all done with the hashtag "living my best life." But the truth is there is a failure on your part and my part to live the best life we could live if we don't pay attention to the distractions in our way. The difference between where you are right now and where you want to be is the way you handle distractions. Distractions will hamper your ability to live your best life.

What's ultimately at stake is your own emotional health. After you've given in to a distraction and satisfied that urge, you won't even be glad you did it. But you will stop thinking about whatever it was you were thinking about—most likely something important.

As it turns out, **the best leaders in the world are the most emotionally healthy people**. This is why it is critical to have a plan to deal with the distractions that will keep you from becoming a better version of you. That is the goal of this study—not only to guide you on how to turn down the distractions but also to help you arrive at that better place.

Notes

Notes

GROUP DISCUSSION

Choose the questions that work best for your group.

1. Do you believe there are more or fewer distractions in the world today than ten years ago? Give a few reasons to support your answer.

2. What are the main things that cause you to lose focus or not remain present to what's going on around you? What draws you to these specific distractions?

3. Journalist Nellie Bowles once said, "Technologists know how phones really work, and many have decided they don't want their own children anywhere near them." How does this quote make you feel? Why?

4. What are the opportunity costs of some of your distractions—in other words, what could you have done or experienced had you spent that time being fully present or pursuing what really matters?

5. Where are you spinning your wheels and stuck in the same routine? What would you like to do if you could gain traction in those areas?

MY LEADERSHIP CHALLENGE

Complete this exercise on your own. Take up to fifteen minutes.

In the space below, name the cost of distractions in the following areas:

Marriage

Children

Work

Hobbies

Rest

Faith

SESSION WRAP-UP

The danger of distraction is real . . . and costly. In this session, we've identified the problem and named what we lose when we allow ourselves to stay distracted. As leaders of ourselves and others, we're responsible for limiting our distractions so we can be present to those around us—from business relationships to family and friends.

PERSONAL STUDY

If you want to enhance your group study experience, consider doing any of the following activities on your own before the next meeting.

READ

Read chapter 1, "The Danger of Distraction," in *How to Lead in a World of Distraction*. Write down some of your key takeaways from this chapter.

DO

Try an experiment. Pick a day to turn off your phone and stay off social media from dinner until the next morning. Notice how much more present you are to those around you and the new opportunities it frees up for you. If it's a positive experience, would you consider making it a daily practice? Why or why not?

Think about some of the devastation and mayhem that a loss of traction can cause when you are driving in snow or a blizzard. Consider this dramatic imagery as you picture areas in your life where you aren't moving forward. Name one strategy for gaining traction that you are willing to try based on this week's study.

REFLECT

Read Matthew 4:1–11:

> Then Jesus was led by the Spirit into the wilderness to be tempted by the devil. After fasting forty days and forty nights, he was hungry. The tempter came

to him and said, "If you are the Son of God, tell these stones to become bread."

Jesus answered, "It is written: 'Man shall not live on bread alone, but on every word that comes from the mouth of God.'"

Then the devil took him to the holy city and had him stand on the highest point of the temple. "If you are the Son of God," he said, "throw yourself down. For it is written:

"'He will command his angels concerning you,
    and they will lift you up in their hands,
    so that you will not strike your foot against a
       stone.'"

Jesus answered him, "It is also written: 'Do not put the Lord your God to the test.'"

Again, the devil took him to a very high mountain and showed him all the kingdoms of the world and their splendor. "All this I will give you," he said, "if you will bow down and worship me."

Jesus said to him, "Away from me, Satan! For it is written: 'Worship the Lord your God, and serve him only.'"

Then the devil left him, and angels came and attended him.

Reflect on these questions:

How did Jesus resist the enemy's temptations to be distracted from his mission? What would have been the cost if he had allowed himself to be distracted from his purpose?

What insights does Jesus' example give about how you can resist distractions in your life?

Read Luke 10:38–42:

As Jesus and his disciples were on their way, he came to a village where a woman named Martha opened her home to him. She had a sister called Mary, who sat at the Lord's feet listening to what he said. But Martha was distracted by all the preparations that had to be made. She came to him and asked, "Lord, don't you care that my sister has left me to do the work by myself? Tell her to help me!"

"Martha, Martha," the Lord answered, "you are worried and upset about many things, but few things are needed—or indeed only one. Mary has chosen what is better, and it will not be taken away from her."

Reflect on these questions:

What do you think Jesus meant when he said that Mary had chosen "what is better"?

What has been a costly personal consequence of your being distracted? When is a time that you—like Martha—risked missing an opportunity because you were distracted?

APPLY

Whom do you trust to offer you honest feedback on your level of distraction? Are you willing to seek that person's input and—without challenging their opinion—simply listen?

TURNING DOWN THE WHITE NOISE

Once I removed that piece of me . . . I realized that sometimes music can act as a distraction and can get in the way of where your mind wants to go.

TYLER JOSEPH,
OF TWENTY ONE PILOTS

SESSION OVERVIEW

White noise is an effective sound-masking tool. It creates a hum of distraction to cover the sounds we don't want to hear. The problem is we can create our own version of "white noise" to cover up feelings we don't want to address. We find a show to binge on when we feel lonely. We shop when we feel anxious. We focus on work because we feel inadequate. The way out is to learn to *name* our noise. Once we understand what we're using to distract us, we can *experiment* with it and learn to *listen* to what the noise is actually masking. Great leaders must turn down the noise low enough and long enough to be ruthlessly curious about their emotions.

CONVERSATION STARTER

Finish the following statement: "Some of the ways I distract myself from having to deal with difficult problems are _____ _____."

VIDEO TEACHING

Watch the video segment for session two. A summary is provided for your benefit as well as space to take additional notes.

Summary

Distractions manage to do two things really well. First, they make promises. They offer us something we want in the moment and promise to help us cope with a difficult challenge. Second, they deliver on their promises. Unlike the classic Ja Rule and Ashanti song, they are *always* there when you call and *always* on time. Distractions make good on their promises . . . even when those promises are quite empty.

There are a few things about white noise that are always true. First, **white noise masks what we don't want to hear.** It creates a hum of soothing distraction to cover up the sounds we don't want to hear. Personally, I like *heavy rain pouring, blowing wind,* and *brown noise.* Those are far and away the best forms of soothing noise for getting optimal sleep. And it's amazing how accessible our phones have made white noise. Many apps now provide this tool and give loads of options for sounds. But the goal is always to mask other sounds.

Second, **white noise is constant.** Try this experiment. Sit still and pay attention to what you can hear. I'll guarantee you will hear something, whether it's the hum of the air conditioner, the traffic outside, the birds chirping, or the breeze blowing through the trees. There is always something for us to hear. It's impossible for us to live life without any noise.

Third, **white noise is really just a form of distraction.** There is a noise you can't hear because of how loud the white noise actually is around you. I appreciate how the band

Twenty One Pilots described it in their song "Car Radio." The storyline behind the song is that a guy had his radio stolen from his car. Now, the noise he used to have while driving is gone . . . and he is forced to wrestle with the fears that have lain dormant inside him. He wants the masking effect of the music to help him stop thinking about the deeper questions he wants to avoid. I have found all of us have our fingers on the dial of some kind of noise we are using to tune out other things. And it is getting in the way of our becoming better people—and better leaders. The good news is that you have control over this. You have your fingers on the knob of that white noise machine in your life. You can choose not to crank it up when anxiety hits, or when you have fears about the future, or when you encounter feelings of inadequacy.

So how do you do this? There are three key steps. First, **name your noise**. When I share these concepts with emerging leaders and ask them to name the most common forms of white noise in their lives, I'm always amazed how similar the answers are. Whether the crowd is a group of business leaders, church leaders, parents of teenagers, or even college students, the most common answers are always *work, television, radio, news, podcasts, exercise, alcohol, eating,* and *shopping*. What is that white noise for you? What do you use to avoid dealing with your feelings and the reality of your situation? Until you identify it, you can't turn it down.

Second, **experiment with your noise**. Self-leadership demands that you know more about yourself than anyone else. In order to become well versed in the ins and outs of yourself, you need to observe and understand the distractions and noises in your life. Think about those things that have become a habit—what others would say is a distraction. Now consider what it would look like to *stop* doing those things. What might it look like to stop making personal purchases for a month, whether new pillows for the couch or another hoodie sweatshirt? What if you went without dessert for a month? What if you didn't binge-watch that particular show you like? Remove the masking mechanism from your life.

Third, **listen to what's there**. Once you've removed the white noise, you can actually hear what it was masking. Remember, you have emotions inside you that will not be addressed until you're aware of them. And you can't be aware of them if the noise in your life is so loud that you can't hear them. Your emotions are messengers that are trying to tell you something. Turning down the white noise—the distractions—will help you know what they are saying. So, to examine your life, name your noise, experiment with turning down the volume, and then listen to what's left in the quiet that follows.

The best kinds of leaders are the most emotionally healthy people. As you learn to turn down the noise low enough and long enough to be ruthlessly curious about your emotions, you'll find that it actually makes you a better person as well.

Notes

Notes

GROUP DISCUSSION

Choose the questions that work best for your group.

1. Distractions promise that if you pay attention to them, you will definitely lose focus on the other thing you were thinking about. Distractions will draw you away from what you should be focusing on. How have you found this to be true in your life?

2. What are the three traits of white noise? What are some common examples of white noise that people use to block out what they don't want to hear?

3. Can you relate to the person who lost his car radio in the Twenty One Pilots song? How does the thought of "having no sound to hide behind" make you feel?

4. Until you identify the noise in your life, you can't turn it down. What is your go-to white noise that hinders you from hearing the sounds you need to hear?

5. We all have emotions inside of us that will not be addressed until we're aware of them—and actively pursue them. What is the biggest internal or external issue that you need to spend focused time on to lead yourself and others better?

MY LEADERSHIP CHALLENGE

Complete this exercise on your own. Take up to fifteen minutes on the first three steps. The final steps will play out over the course of the next week . . . so be patient and stay observant!

We're going to do an experiment with your noise that involves the scientific method. Now, I realize it may have been high school or college since you were last in a science class. That's okay. There won't be a test on this. But I've found the scientific method is a great way to help us better understand our dependence on white noise. With this in mind, follow each of the steps listed below as it relates to the white noise in your life.

Step 1: Observe
Name what your "go-to" white noise tends to be.

Step 2: Hypothesize
Make an assumption about what the real issue is that you're using the white noise to mask.

Step 3: Change a Variable

Now think about what you can do differently as it relates to how you approach this issue. This might involve adopting a new behavior, or practicing better self-talk, or directly addressing a person or situation. The goal is to see how the new variable could lead to a new outcome.

Step 4: Test

This week look for ways to put the new variable into action so you can test whether your hypothesis is correct. Write down your findings in the space below.

Step 5: Repeat

If your testing determined that your hypothesis was true, it's time to evaluate and course-correct. This is rarely a one-and-done process, but rather a journey of discovery. Continue to observe, hypothesize, change a variable, test, and repeat until you reach victory in this area of your life. In the space below, write down some ways you will do this.

SESSION WRAP-UP

We all use white noise in our lives to avoid dealing directly with our feelings. But the truth is the longer we rely on the noise, the longer we refuse to attend to our feelings—and the less emotionally healthy we become. The solution is to quiet the noise to gain clarity—to name your noise, experiment with it, and listen to what it was masking. One way good leaders become great leaders is by being ruthlessly curious about their emotions and investing in their emotional well-being. Self-leadership demands that you know more about yourself than anyone else.

PERSONAL STUDY

If you want to enhance your group study experience, consider doing any of the following activities on your own before the next meeting.

READ

Read chapter 2, "White Noise," in *How to Lead in a World of Distraction*. Also review chapter 3, "The Three Villains of Leadership," and chapter 4, "The Me of Leadership." The content of these chapters, though not covered during this week's meeting, reveals three distractions that have the strongest gravitational pull on a leader's attention as well as how to become an "emotional detective." Write down some of your key takeaways from these chapters.

DO

Music has a simple power to reveal truth, so this week, listen to the song "Car Radio" by Twenty One Pilots. How do the lyrics speak to you about the ways we use white noise to mask our deeper desires and emotions? If helpful, use specific lines from the song to make your points.

Watch the TED Talk "Listening to Shame" by Brené Brown. How does she describe the difference between *guilt* and *shame*? How might understanding this difference help you to process your emotions as you seek to become a more effective leader?

REFLECT

Read Genesis 3:1–10:

Now the serpent was more crafty than any of the wild animals the Lord God had made. He said to the woman, "Did God really say, 'You must not eat from any tree in the garden'?"

The woman said to the serpent, "We may eat fruit from the trees in the garden, but God did say, 'You must not eat fruit from the tree that is in the middle of the garden, and you must not touch it, or you will die.' "

"You will not certainly die," the serpent said to the woman. "For God knows that when you eat from it your eyes will be opened, and you will be like God, knowing good and evil."

When the woman saw that the fruit of the tree was good for food and pleasing to the eye, and also desirable for gaining wisdom, she took some and ate it. She also gave some to her husband, who was with her, and he ate it. Then the eyes of both of them were opened, and they realized they were naked; so they sewed fig leaves together and made coverings for themselves.

Then the man and his wife heard the sound of the Lord God as he was walking in the garden in the cool of the day, and they hid from the Lord God among the trees of the garden. But the Lord God called to the man, "Where are you?"

He answered, "I heard you in the garden, and I was afraid because I was naked; so I hid."

Reflect on these questions:

What was Adam and Eve's first instinct when they realized they had sinned?

What are some ways people "hide" today when they don't want to deal with guilt and painful emotions?

Read Luke 8:42–48:

As Jesus was on his way, the crowds almost crushed him. And a woman was there who had been subject to bleeding for twelve years, but no one could heal her. She came up behind him and touched the edge of his cloak, and immediately her bleeding stopped.

"Who touched me?" Jesus asked.

When they all denied it, Peter said, "Master, the people are crowding and pressing against you."

But Jesus said, "Someone touched me; I know that power has gone out from me."

Then the woman, seeing that she could not go unnoticed, came trembling and fell at his feet. In the presence of all the people, she told why she had touched him and how she had been instantly healed. Then he said to her, "Daughter, your faith has healed you. Go in peace."

Reflect on these questions:

Why did the woman approach Jesus in the way that she did? How did she react when she realized her actions could not go unnoticed?

How did Jesus restore the woman? How has he likewise restored you?

APPLY

In order to become a master of self-awareness, you need to observe and understand the white noise in your life. What are some habits you have developed to avoid dealing with difficult situations or emotions? Are you willing to experiment by not doing those habits for a month?

FINDING
SIMPLICITY

All well-drawn characters have a spine: an inner motor, a dominant, unconscious goal that they're striving for, an itch they can't scratch.

ANDREW STANTON,
FROM "THE CLUES TO A GREAT STORY"

SESSION OVERVIEW

Just as noise-reducing headphones cancel out distracting sounds in our world, four key practices can help us identify and reduce the noise in our lives. The first is the practice of *finding simplicity*, which can enable us to break through the inner clutter in our heart and find our supreme motivation. This is essential, because the more we can simplify our interior world, the more we'll be able to navigate the busy demands of the exterior world around us.

CONVERSATION STARTER

Finish the following statement: "The key driving force in my life—the one thing that motivates me and keeps me moving forward—is _____ _____."

VIDEO TEACHING

Watch the video segment for session three. A summary is provided for your benefit as well as space to take additional notes.

Summary

Have you ever used a pair of noise-canceling headphones? These feats of audio magic actually seek out frequencies to block. Then, once they find an unwanted frequency, they create their own sound waves to mimic the incoming noise—with the exception that the waves they produce are about 180 degrees out of phase with the intruding waves. This means the headphones effectively block out about 70 percent of ambient noise.

We all need "noise-canceling headphones" when it comes to distractions. We need to employ habits that *cancel out* the distractions that are interfering with our emotional health—and keeping us from growing as leaders, parents, friends, teachers, counselors, and the other roles we take on each day. The good news is that such habits exist. **There are habits we can leverage in our lives that can become noise-canceling habits.** The best part is these habits, unlike noise-canceling headphones, are free. Actually, it's *not* using them that is costly.

As we discuss these habits, I want to get practical. Up to this point, I've been working to give you a vision for why it is important to deal with the distractions in your life. I hope I've convinced you. But the real work will begin when you start to *use* the tools that I am about to provide to deal with these distractions. The first one is simple . . . quite literally. In fact, the habit we are going to discuss is *finding simplicity*. It's about finding out your most basic drive in life—the thing that motivates you the most.

Andrew Stanton, the Oscar-winning filmmaker behind many Pixar classics, said that when it comes to creating a compelling character in a story, that character has to have a *spine*. In other words, the character has to have a dominant and unconscious goal they're striving to reach. The same is true of us . . . and we all have such goals. Deep within us, there is something that pushes us to do the things we do and to behave the way we behave.

Simplicity is the practice that will help you uncover that goal. **The more simple your life, the more able you are to identify your *why*. And the more able you are to identify your *why*, the more able you are to simplify your life.** They work together. This is so important, because when you can clarify your *why*, you can start to live and lead effectively. Finding the *why* will help you find the traction in life that builds momentum and minimize the pull of distractions.

Yet simplicity can be difficult to find in today's world. Not only is there so much clutter in our world today, but there is also so much clutter in our physical lives. We live in a world that just loves more. We want to supersize everything. If we're honest, most of our lives are crammed full of stuff, maybe even to the point that we can't open the door without things falling out. That's why we have to be intentional about finding simplicity. **We need to declutter our physical lives, but we also need to declutter our emotional lives as well.**

Jesus said, "Blessed are the pure in heart, for they will see God" (Matthew 5:8). He makes a brilliant connection between the purity of our heart—how simple our inner world is—and how that enables us to see God. I imagine that every one of us, if we could see what God sees, would *want* to see like God does. Jesus says there is a connection between the purity in our heart and our ability to see God or even see like God. **The more clutter we have in our lives, the less able we are to fight for and find simplicity.**

The reason this is such an important concept to self-leadership is because only *you* know what's most important to you. Only you really can know what that thing is inside of you that's driving you. So the question is . . . **do you know your why?** Do you know the thing that motivates you? Can you eliminate all of the other things around you that are trying to grab your attention, or grab your control, or even grab your heart?

Here's my challenge: *Simplify what's important to you in every aspect of your life.* Know why you do what you do. After all, you can't clean out your closet until you know why you're doing it. The *why* becomes your filter for making the tough decisions of what to do and what to drop, what to keep and what to give away.

When you clarify your why, you have a filter to simplify your life. This won't magically make those normal, boring day-to-day tasks go away. There will still be phone calls, emails, and those annoying tasks. Those things still need to happen. But when you clarify your why, you see these things in a new light—through the lens of how they support what ultimately matters.

Notes

Notes

GROUP DISCUSSION

Choose the questions that work best for your group.

1. Does the thought of simplifying your life appeal to you? Why or why not?

2. Just as our physical lives have clutter, so do our inner lives. What specific areas of your inner life feel overly cluttered at this moment?

3. What are some items, meetings, or tasks you could get rid of? What would you say are your essentials?

4. Your emotions are like messengers. What have they been trying to tell you? Can you name a distraction that has kept you from hearing this message?

5. It is important to be "ruthlessly curious" about your emotions. How would you rate your emotional well-being on a scale from 1 (not at all curious) to 5 (ruthlessly curious)? What level would you prefer to be? Why?

MY LEADERSHIP CHALLENGE

Complete this exercise on your own. Take up to fifteen minutes.

The practice of simplicity boils down to knowing *why* you do what you do. The *why* becomes your filter for making tough decisions and determining what is important to keep in your life and what you need to let go. With this in mind, the following exercise will provide you with a practical way to begin this process of prioritization. I call it "the moose and the monkeys." (Stay with me here.)

Step 1: Make a List of Your Day

Begin by spending a few minutes making a list of everything you did yesterday (for example, *went to the grocery store, met with a colleague, took a class, picked up after the kids*).

Now circle the items that moved you forward *personally* or *professionally*. If nothing jumps out from the list, write down something you *wish* you had done and circle it.

Step 2: Identify the Monkeys

The items you didn't circle are your *monkeys*. These are the less significant things that come up during the day that take up your time and energy. Can you identify two or three of these that don't need chasing? Things you can delegate? Write them in the space below.

Step 3: Identify the Moose

The items you did circle are your *moose*. These are the tasks that represent your top priorities. Can you pick two or three that you want to chase this week? Write them below.

Step 4: Develop a Plan

As a final step, take a few minutes to come up with a plan for how you will stop chasing the monkeys and start pursuing the moose. For the *monkeys*, decide which tasks you can drop, which you can delegate to others, and which—if they have to be done by you—you can bundle together to do on just one day of the week. Bundling tasks in this manner and turning them into one big goal can help you keep the monkeys from derailing each day during the week.

For the *moose*, pick three items at most that you will pursue today. Keep this simple and realistic. Your goal is to take it slow and start the process of prioritizing your daily tasks.

SESSION WRAP-UP

The habit of simplicity starts by understanding your *personal* why. Once you discover this, you can then look at your *professional* why—the reason behind your daily tasks and goals. Clarifying your *why* gives you a filter to simplify your life. This won't make all your tedious tasks go away—there will still be "monkeys" to chase. But it will help you identify those important goals and tasks—the "moose"—and give you a plan for pursuing them. Furthermore, once you've clarified your *why*, you can see both your *monkeys* and your *moose* in a new light—through the lens of how they support what ultimately matters to you as an individual and as a leader.

PERSONAL STUDY

If you want to enhance your group study experience, consider doing any of the following activities on your own before the next meeting.

READ

Read chapter 5, "Noise-Canceling Habits," and chapter 6, "Finding Simplicity," in *How to Lead in a World of Distraction*. Write down some of your key takeaways from these chapters.

DO

Steve Jobs, the founder of Apple, adhered to a principle of simplicity in everything he did. Do a Google or YouTube search and look at the clothes he is wearing—chances are you will see him in a black turtleneck, jeans, and white sneakers. What similar kinds of counterintuitive changes would you be willing to make so you can focus more on just the important decisions in life?

Watch Andrew Stanton's TED Talk titled "The Clues to a Great Story," where he makes the case for simplicity in creating compelling Pixar characters. How does this same principle apply to the power of simplicity in your own life?

REFLECT

Read Matthew 6:25–34:

> Therefore I tell you, do not worry about your life, what you will eat or drink; or about your body, what you will wear. Is not life more than food, and the

body more than clothes? Look at the birds of the air; they do not sow or reap or store away in barns, and yet your heavenly Father feeds them. Are you not much more valuable than they? Can any one of you by worrying add a single hour to your life?

And why do you worry about clothes? See how the flowers of the field grow. They do not labor or spin. Yet I tell you that not even Solomon in all his splendor was dressed like one of these. If that is how God clothes the grass of the field, which is here today and tomorrow is thrown into the fire, will he not much more clothe you—you of little faith? So do not worry, saying, "What shall we eat?" or "What shall we drink?" or "What shall we wear?" For the pagans run after all these things, and your heavenly Father knows that you need them. But seek first his kingdom and his righteousness, and all these things will be given to you as well. Therefore do not worry about tomorrow, for tomorrow will worry about itself. Each day has enough trouble of its own.

Reflect on these questions:

What does Jesus say about worrying in this passage—especially about things out of your control? What does he say your life priorities should be?

What are some things that you are worrying about today? How does this passage encourage you to trust those worries to God's care?

Read 1 Timothy 6:6–12:

But godliness with contentment is great gain. For we brought nothing into the world, and we can take nothing out of it. But if we have food and clothing, we will be content with that. Those who want to get rich fall into temptation and a trap and into many foolish and harmful desires that plunge people into ruin and destruction. For the love of money is a root of all kinds of evil. Some people, eager for money, have wandered from the faith and pierced themselves with many griefs. But you, man of God, flee from all this, and pursue righteousness, godliness, faith, love, endurance and gentleness. Fight the good fight of the faith.

Reflect on these questions:

What does Paul say are the dangers of prioritizing the things of this world?

What simpler things in life does Paul advise us to pursue?

APPLY

King Solomon wrote, "Like a city whose walls are broken through is a person who lacks self-control" (Proverbs 25:28). What part of your internal world resembles a city without walls right now? How might fortifying this area help your emotional health?

SPEAKING TO
YOURSELF

People who are emotionally adept—who know and manage their feelings well, and who read and deal effectively with other people's feelings—are at an advantage in any domain in life.

DANIEL GOLEMAN,
FROM *EMOTIONAL INTELLIGENCE*

SESSION OVERVIEW

If simplicity is finding your *why*, then self-talk is about finding your *way*. Self-talk involves learning to speak words of encouragement to yourself at the beginning of the day, throughout the day, and at the end of the day. In fact, understanding how to converse with yourself in a healthy way is one of the greatest strategies for turning down the noise, picking yourself up, and pointing yourself in the right direction. It is immensely empowering, because it reveals that you don't have to be taken down by distractions or limited by the voice inside your head.

CONVERSATION STARTER

Finish the following statement: "Some of the ways I need to better encourage myself throughout the day are _____ _____."

VIDEO TEACHING

Watch the video segment for session four. A summary is provided for your benefit as well as space to take additional notes.

Summary

As we saw in the previous session, there are practices we can put into place to turn down the noise and develop our emotional health—which is important, because the best leaders are the most emotionally healthy people. The first practice we discussed is finding simplicity. Today, we will discuss the second habit: *speaking to yourself.*

The irony of speaking to yourself is that if not used correctly, it can incidentally *add* to the noise. You talk to yourself all day long, but the messages you're giving yourself are not always trustworthy. The voice inside your head has power. It can control your day by discouraging and demotivating you . . . or it can encourage you and empower you. The good news is that it is up to you how you use it. **You are able to turn down the noise.**

I like the language King David uses in Psalm 42, because he shows us how to speak to ourselves at the beginning of the day, throughout the day, and even at the end of the day. He begins by admitting that he is not in a good place. But then he looks in the mirror and speaks to himself. He tells himself to put his hope in God and celebrate him. David is modeling a practice that allows us to turn down the noise of the other voices we hear during the day.

Speaking to yourself is a crucial habit, because it's the **longest and most robust conversation you will have all day.** Daniel Goleman, who has shaped much of the learning around the topic of emotional intelligence, has been a leading voice on the subject of self-talk. In a recent interview, he discussed how the art of speaking to yourself is essential for business leaders—to the point where it's now one of the factors that defines a person's success.

Goleman points out that emotionally intelligent people are adept at self-narrating their lives. We all have a voice inside our heads telling us what to do, and that voice is listening to other voices—other people around us, things we read or watch, and even reflections we have on our own experiences. We have to make a deliberate choice to serve as the gatekeepers and allow only what's good to come in, making sure the unhelpful stays out, and knowing when to give ourselves a break from all the input.

Learning to explore what's going on inside of us is such a helpful practice. We live in a world where everyone gets a trophy. In any sport my kids have played, they get a trophy just for participating. But if we **self-affirm without self-evaluating, it leads to self-deception**. We begin to deceive ourselves into behaving in a way that is contrary to what we believe.

There are two practices we can use to foster positive self-talk so we can accurately evaluate what is going on in our lives. The first involves **what we tell ourselves as soon as we wake up in the morning.** Self-talk snowballs. So, if the first thing you do in the morning is check your emails, watch the news, and add things to your calendar, you'll be overwhelmed before you get out of bed. Instead, set up your day the night before. Scheduling your time in this manner gives you the power to control your self-talk from the moment you wake up. When you know the day has already been taken care of, you have the freedom to take care of yourself before the day begins.

The second practice is to **ask self-regulating questions throughout the day**. When you set up your day the night before, choose the one thing that has to get done (the moose) before you let any distractions (the monkeys) into your head. Ask yourself, "Is this something only I can do, or would someone else benefit from the opportunity?" I also like the question, "Why am I really saying yes to this?" The first question forces you to think about delegating tasks. The second forces you to think about how you are leading yourself.

Another question I've heard is, **"What would a great leader do?"** You may not always know what a great leader would do in your situation, but training yourself to ask the question will open your mind to see the possibility that you behave like a great leader more than you realize. I also like, **"What advice would you give yourself?"** This allows you to get outside yourself and objectively analyze the situation.

If you start your day with positive self-talk and intersperse self-regulating questions throughout the day, the only thing left is to end with more positive self-talk. If that sounds too good to be true, try it and see. Self-talk will help your days be more productive and positive.

Notes

Notes

GROUP DISCUSSION

Choose the questions that work best for your group.

1. The habit of simplicity is about finding your *why*, while self-talk is about finding your *way*. How would you describe the differences between these two habits?

2. The invisible internal habits you practice will bring the most visible external results. What example of this can you give from your life?

3. The voice inside your head has the power to discourage
   and demotivate you or encourage and empower you.
   Which have you experienced more in the past week?
   How did it affect your attitude and mindset?

4. What is your routine like in the morning? How do you
   think starting your day with positive self-talk would
   impact the rest of your day?

5. What are some self-regulating questions you need to
   ask when it comes to your schedule and your
   commitments?

MY LEADERSHIP CHALLENGE

Complete this exercise on your own. Take up to fifteen minutes.

There are several questions you can ask yourself throughout the day to separate your important goals (your moose) from your tedious distractions (your monkeys). Think about what tomorrow looks like for you—the tasks you have to complete, goals you need to meet, appointments you need to schedule, and the like. Write a few of these in the space below.

Now evaluate which of these items really need to be on your calendar, why you are doing them, and which you can delegate to others. Use the following questions to guide you.

What is motivating me to say yes to this task or this opportunity?

Is there someone else who can do this? If so, how would it benefit that person?

Take a few moments to get outside yourself and objectively analyze your situation. Think about one key task in particular as you use the following questions to guide you.

What is one challenge or goal that I need to handle tomorrow? What would a *great* leader do in my situation to handle that issue?

What advice would I give to someone else who was facing this challenge or goal?

SESSION WRAP-UP

It's true that the voice inside your head has power over you. But you have power over that voice. Most of us recognize the first part—we know negative thoughts can put a damper on our day while positive thoughts can brighten it. Few of us acknowledge the second part. This is a mistake, because when we control the noise, we limit the power of our negative thoughts and increase the power of our positive thoughts. So we need to make it a point to talk to ourselves—to slow down and ask self-regulating questions. The regular practice of self-talk will help us become more effective leaders as well as better spouses, parents, coworkers, and people in general.

PERSONAL STUDY

If you want to enhance your group study experience, consider doing any of the following activities on your own before the next meeting.

READ

Read chapter 7, "Speaking to Yourself," in *How to Lead in a World of Distraction*. Write down some of your key takeaways from this chapter.

DO

In the movie *Stranger Than Fiction*, Will Ferrell plays an unstable IRS auditor who hears the voice of an author (played by Emma Thompson) inside his head and comes to discover he is the protagonist in her latest work. Watch or read a review of this film. How does this story reveal the impact of the voices in our heads? What power do you have to change the voices?

Find your favorite translation of Psalm 42 and read it out loud. Listen to David's expressive language and get a sense of his emotional state. Notice also the practice he exemplifies of naming his feelings, acknowledging his negative self-talk, and then holding on to what he knows is true. Follow David's example by taking a few minutes for introspection. What has you upset or feeling down? What negative words is your inner voice telling you? What affirming words can you hold on to today to counter this negative self-talk?

REFLECT

Read Philippians 3:7–14:

> But whatever were gains to me I now consider loss
> for the sake of Christ. What is more, I consider

everything a loss because of the surpassing worth of knowing Christ Jesus my Lord, for whose sake I have lost all things. I consider them garbage, that I may gain Christ and be found in him, not having a righteousness of my own that comes from the law, but that which is through faith in Christ—the righteousness that comes from God on the basis of faith. I want to know Christ—yes, to know the power of his resurrection and participation in his sufferings, becoming like him in his death, and so, somehow, attaining to the resurrection from the dead.

Not that I have already obtained all this, or have already arrived at my goal, but I press on to take hold of that for which Christ Jesus took hold of me. Brothers and sisters, I do not consider myself yet to have taken hold of it. But one thing I do: Forgetting what is behind and straining toward what is ahead, I press on toward the goal to win the prize for which God has called me heavenward in Christ Jesus.

Reflect on these questions:

How does Paul demonstrate that he clearly understands his priorities? What does he say to himself to help him keep striving toward his goals?

In what areas of your life do you need to "forget what is behind"? What do you need to tell yourself today to keep you "straining toward what is ahead"?

Read 2 Corinthians 4:8–18:

We are hard pressed on every side, but not crushed; perplexed, but not in despair; persecuted, but not abandoned; struck down, but not destroyed. We always carry around in our body the death of Jesus, so that the life of Jesus may also be revealed in our body. For we who are alive are always being given over to death for Jesus' sake, so that his life may also be revealed in our mortal body. So then, death is at work in us, but life is at work in you.

It is written: "I believed; therefore I have spoken." Since we have that same spirit of faith, we also believe and therefore speak, because we know that the one who raised the Lord Jesus from the dead will also raise us with Jesus and present us with you to himself. All this is for your benefit, so that the grace that is reaching more and more people may cause thanksgiving to overflow to the glory of God.

Therefore we do not lose heart. Though outwardly we are wasting away, yet inwardly we are being renewed day by day. For our light and momentary troubles are achieving for us an eternal glory that far outweighs them all. So we fix our eyes not on what is seen, but on what is unseen, since what is seen is temporary, but what is unseen is eternal.

Reflect on these questions:

What difficulties does Paul say he is facing? How has he chosen to respond?

What truths do you need to speak today to reassure yourself that God is in control and is with you in your difficult times?

APPLY

Great leaders are always thinking and always asking questions . . . and we need to learn from their example. Who are some people you consider to be great leaders in your life? Would you be willing this week to seek their advice for a situation you are facing?

GETTING
QUIET

Culture conditions us to be comfortable with noise and crowds, not with silence and solitude, and to feel more at home in a mall than at a park.

DONALD WHITNEY,
FROM *SPIRITUAL DISCIPLINES FOR THE CHRISTIAN LIFE*

SESSION OVERVIEW

Many people are uncomfortable with the silence that solitude brings. Yet getting quiet is an essential practice we need to develop if we want to lead in a world of distraction. Every day we are continually bombarded by information—emails, texts, tweets, social media posts, and the like. Staying informed and communicating with others are healthy facets of life, but if we never get a break to be by ourselves, we'll never learn to think. In the same way speaking to ourselves helps us better understand the voice inside our heads, getting quiet will help us to know ourselves better. And when we understand who we are, we can then better understand and lead others.

CONVERSATION STARTER

Finish the following statement: "Spending time in silence and solitude is difficult for me because _____
_____."

VIDEO TEACHING

Watch the video segment for session five. A summary is provided for your benefit as well as space to take additional notes.

Summary

None of us is comfortable with complete silence. It's why solitary confinement is such an effective punishment for disruptive prison inmates. In fact, if you tried to sit in perfect silence for a length of time, it would make you go crazy. But silence can be powerful when it comes to your emotional health. It can help you to **turn down the noise so you can be ruthlessly curious about your own emotions**. And it comes from getting quiet on a regular basis.

In a study done by EmotionallyHealthy.org, researchers brought in sets of parents and adult kids to have them experience the power of emotional silence. They were taken into a sterile room, one parent-child pair at a time, and asked to stand facing each other—perfectly quiet and perfectly still—for *four* full minutes. The results are amazing. A mother tells how she looked into her son's face and thought about the moment he was born. A son tells of how much gratitude he felt when he thought about all his mother had sacrificed for him. A father tells of how much potential he sees in his daughter's future.

It's such a simple but profound concept. I'm telling you, **if you're going to be an emotionally healthy person and leader, getting quiet has to be a part of your life**. And it can't be a one-time thing. It must become part of your daily (or at least weekly) routine.

A friend of mine emailed about thirty CEOs and asked what morning habits they had that made them successful.

One of the most common responses he received was, "If something's important, you've got to get it done before lunch. If it's really important, you've got to get it done before breakfast." The second most common response was that the CEOs took time to be alone, to be quiet, and to experience solitude for the sake of reflection.

I think many of us today are missing out on this crucial practice of silence and solitude . . . and we are paying the price. But, of course, we have jobs, families, friends, and responsibilities, and it can be tough to *escape* from them to a place of isolation. So instead, we need to learn how to *get away* from noise at appropriate times and in a healthy way. We need to find a place, find a time, and get a plan.

First, **find a place**. At this stage with my young family, there are many things I have to be flexible about. But I have one constant every morning: my desk. After coffee, my desk is the first place I go to get my day started. The great thing is that I can make it my own. Likewise, your place doesn't have to be anything special. It just has to be a place dedicated to noise-free reflection. And it has to be a place you can return to regularly.

Second, **find a time**. Your place needs to be somewhere you go every day, and the way you instill this habit is by picking a time to practice it. Most people prefer mornings, as it allows them to see the positive effect that spending time in solitude has on their mindset for the day. Maybe for you this is your morning commute. It's amazing how powerful that drive can be if you have nothing else going on besides your thoughts, your emotions, and your opportunity to discover what's going on inside of you. Again, the key is consistency.

Third, **get a plan**. If you haven't noticed, the key to successfully getting quiet is *you*—and it can be difficult to guide your thoughts when you're in solitude. This is why you need a plan. Journaling can be an excellent way to structure your time, as it allows you to dump your thoughts and emotions on paper. For me, I write down three things I want, I need, and I surrender. This allows the silence and solitude to be guided. You just have to find out what works best for you and commit yourself to following through on the practice.

Finally, **I would advise to keep it low and take it slow**. Anyone who has dabbled in smoking meat knows there are two important objectives: you have to keep the temperature low, and you have to take it slow. The same is true with silence and solitude. Keep the noise low, and don't bite off more than you can chew. Just start with two minutes of solitude at the start of your day. Work your way up. If you do, you'll find it can become a meaningful lifelong habit that will help you lead like you want to lead even in this extraordinarily distracted world.

Notes

GROUP DISCUSSION

Choose the questions that work best for your group.

1. How would you describe the difference between *silence* and *solitude*? When was the last time you experienced each of them?

2. How have you witnessed the power of silence and solitude in your life? When are times you have made significant changes in your life because of such reflection?

3. Where is a place you could routinely go for solitude? When could you do it? What about this place and time would make it ideal for getting away from distractions?

4. What is your plan for spending this time in solitude? How do you think having a plan will make you a better person and a better leader?

5. What is your strategy for starting this plan today? How will you take it slow as you seek to keep the noise low?

MY LEADERSHIP CHALLENGE

Complete this exercise on your own. Take up to fifteen minutes.

This week's challenge is less about doing and more about being. Find a quiet space away from your group members to do this exercise. Feel free to go into a separate room if needed. Silence your phone and set a timer for ten minutes. Sit silently until the alarm goes off. Don't distract yourself with reading, journaling, or anything else. Simply remain in solitude. Once the alarm has gone off, answer the following questions.

Were you comfortable or uncomfortable with this time of silence? Why?

What distractions did you confront? How did you address these distractions?

What thoughts, emotions, or insights came to you during this time?

Would you be willing to make silence and solitude a daily practice? Or did you find you need to have a more structured plan for this time—such as journaling? Explain.

How do you think a regular time of self-inspection would make you a better leader?

SESSION WRAP-UP

If you want to be a good leader, you need to know who you are and what you're about. One of the best ways to do this is to routinely step away from the noise and spend time alone. *Solitude* implies being alone long enough to learn who you are. As you do this, you'll be practicing something completely against cultural norms. The noise of the world doesn't want you to hear yourself. Every day, you'll be able to think of something better to do with that time rather than spending it in solitude and silence. But practicing this habit will free you to be a better leader—and someone who isn't constantly drowning in the same noise everyone else hears.

PERSONAL STUDY

If you want to enhance your group study experience, consider doing any of the following activities on your own before the next meeting.

READ

Read chapter 8, "Getting Quiet," in *How to Lead in a World of Distraction*. Write down some of your key takeaways from this chapter.

DO

Go on YouTube and search for a project called "The Bridge: Face to Face" posted by the Jubilee Project. (You can also find the video in the article "Face to Face: Parents, Children Share Four Minutes of Emotional Silence," posted by NBC News.) Watch the video and notice how the pair are uncomfortable at first, but then there's a transition to something profound. How do you think silence makes this experience possible?

Take a look at the description for the Calm app created by Apple. What does it say that the company responsible for so many people spending so much time on their iPhones and devices sees value in an app that helps turn down the noise?

REFLECT

Read Mark 1:35–39:

> Very early in the morning, while it was still dark, Jesus got up, left the house and went off to a solitary place, where he prayed. Simon and his companions went to look for him, and when they found him, they exclaimed: "Everyone is looking for you!"
>
> Jesus replied, "Let us go somewhere else—to the nearby villages—so I can preach there also. That is why I have come." So he traveled throughout Galilee, preaching in their synagogues and driving out demons.

Reflect on these questions:

What do you learn in this passage about Jesus' practices regarding prayer and solitude?

How do you think this time of solitude focused Jesus' thoughts? How do you see him responding to the disciples' cry that everyone was looking for him?

Read Mark 6:30–34:

> The apostles gathered around Jesus and reported to him all they had done and taught. Then, because so many people were coming and going that they did not even have a chance to eat, he said to them, "Come with me by yourselves to a quiet place and get some rest."
>
> So they went away by themselves in a boat to a solitary place. But many who saw them leaving recognized them and ran on foot from all the towns and got there ahead of them. When Jesus landed and saw a large crowd, he had compassion on them, because they were like sheep without a shepherd. So he began teaching them many things.

Reflect on these questions:

Why did Jesus feel the disciples needed to get away from the crowds and spend time in a solitary place?

What do you see as the importance of getting away from the "crowds" at times and just spending some moments in solitude?

APPLY

To grow comfortable with times of silence and solitude, it helps to have a guided experience. This week try the exercise mentioned during the group time. Get a piece of paper and write down these questions: (1) What do you most want right now? (2) What do you most need right now? (3) What do you feel led to surrender right now? Find a place with no distractions or competing voices and record your answers during your time of solitude.

SESSION 6

PRESSING PAUSE

Life moves pretty fast. If you don't stop and look around once in a while, you might miss it.

FERRIS BUELLER,
FROM *FERRIS BUELLER'S DAY OFF*

SESSION OVERVIEW

So far in this study, we've discussed the habits of *finding simplicity, speaking to yourself,* and *getting quiet.* This last session covers the final habit—*pressing pause.* As you've likely noticed, the habits we've covered will create tendencies that make you different. Finding your *why* fights against our culture's glorification of materialism and busyness. Few voices in the world preach the value of pressing pause. But as we will see, it is a powerful habit that can lead to greater emotional health—and make us better leaders in a world of distraction.

CONVERSATION STARTER

Finish the following statement: "The idea of fasting from food or social media makes me feel _____
_____."

VIDEO TEACHING

Watch the video segment for session six. A summary is provided for your benefit as well as space to take additional notes.

Summary

Finding simplicity. Speaking to yourself. Getting quiet. None of these practices are ingenious, but neither are they considered normal in our world today. However, if you want to be a leader who leads like no one else, you must learn to live like no one else. In this final session, I want to encourage you to make a decision to do something *different* from what the world says to turn down the noise. This is because **what's on the other side—discovery, exploration, evaluation, and growth—are things you won't experience any other way.**

The final habit of *pressing pause* is powerful in our quest for personal growth. But to understand its power, we have to understand why the habit of Sabbath has stood the test of time. For thousands of years, cultures have instituted and instilled the value of taking breaks from work for the sake of rest and reflection. The word may carry strong religious overtones, but the philosophy of the practice of Sabbath appears in almost every culture around the world. It is not only about Sunday. It's a personal discipline for the sake of becoming healthier.

The Sabbath has existed from the beginning of creation. After God made everything, he took a day of rest. This wasn't because God was tired but to set a precedent for his people to follow. God designed rest to be a part of our nature. He made us so we would need a day off. This rule, this guideline, was a model for living that would benefit all who practiced it.

The habit of fasting is also a means to press pause. Fasting from anything—whether food, social media, shopping, or work—is a practical way to implement the principles of Sabbath in many areas of life. Fasting can be a way to turn down the noise in order to spark emotional curiosity. In these two practices—Sabbath and fasting—we see this brilliant and simple idea of saying, "You know what? Life is going to continue without me for a little while, but I'm going to press pause for an hour, a day, a week, or maybe even a month, because of what could happen inside of me if I don't turn down the noise."

Pressing pause really is about finding rhythm. It is not simply a way to quit things. It's also a way to start something new—a healthier life rhythm. Now, rhythm is not to be confused with *balance*. Balance is all about trying to juggle many things—work, family, finances, health, fitness—and keep all the balls in the air. It's a hard practice to maintain over any length of time, but finding a *rhythm* of pressing pause in life is more realistic. With this in mind, I want to give you three reasons why finding a rhythm of pressing pause is so helpful.

First, **rhythm is a reminder**. There is something about a rhythm of pressing pause that we just wouldn't be reminded about in any other way. Taking a Sabbath can remind us that our work doesn't actually depend on us. We just play the *role* of our professions. Likewise, going on a fast from certain things can remind us of their purpose in the first place. For example, giving up sweets can remind us that we have them in our lives to remind us to slow down and enjoy the simple things. Or the fast might reveal we are eating too many sweets.

Second, **rhythm is something we do to remember**. Think back to when we talked about finding your *why*. Sometimes, there's too much noise in the world to truly answer the question, "Why am I doing this?" But finding space away from all the distractions can give us the chance to find our why. In our careers, it can give us the opportunity to stop and remember why we took the job. It allows you to remember what you believe, what your values are, and what is really important to you. The shift is subtle, but it's huge.

Third, **rhythm is something we do to replenish**. We try to do everything we can at work, at home, and in our hobbies—but we simply don't have the time or energy to do everything well. Pressing pause is a way to make space to replenish ourselves and eliminate the amount of distractions. If we don't take time to refill our tank, we won't have anything to pour out to others. If we only fill ourselves up with noise, what we pour out won't do anybody else any good.

Pressing pause is about intentionally stopping the constant demands and expectations of life in a strategic and thoughtful way. It provides the space to remember what's really important to you, remind yourself of your why, and then replenish. When you find this new rhythm, you'll see the world, your purpose, your priorities, and yourself in a whole new light.

Notes

Notes

GROUP DISCUSSION

Choose the questions that work best for your group.

1. Which of these habits—finding simplicity, speaking to yourself, getting quiet, and pressing pause—comes most naturally to you? Which is hardest for you?

2. Most self-help practices are based on current trends and fads. How does it affect you to know that the habit of pressing pause is an ancient practice that has been embraced by almost every culture and set in motion by God himself on the seventh day of creation?

3. Pressing pause is really about finding rhythm in life. Based on this week's teaching, how would you articulate the difference between rhythm and balance? Why is rhythm more realistic and helpful than balance in turning down the noise?

4. How can a rhythm of pressing pause serve to remind you of who you are—and that your life is not defined by your job? How can it help you remember what is truly important to you in life and why you pursued a certain career in the first place?

5. How can a rhythm of pressing pause help you replenish? How have you seen that taking a break actually helps you to be more productive?

6. Where in life do you need to press pause and take a Sabbath break? What are some things you need to give up for a time so you can discover what's going on inside of you? How will you intentionally press pause this week?

MY LEADERSHIP CHALLENGE

Complete this exercise on your own. Take up to fifteen minutes to answer the questions. The final steps will play out over the course of the next week . . . so be patient and stay observant!

This final challenge is to pick something to quit for a week. This is not necessarily because it is bad; rather, the goal is to give something up in order to develop other strengths. You're choosing to turn down the noise so you can hear someone else. You're choosing not to do something so that you can rest. It's not usually easy, but it is purposeful. To help you determine what to quit for a week, spend time with the following questions:

What are the areas of life where you need a break?

What keeps you from finding rest?

How can you take time away from that thing?

What do you think the benefits will be?

Be sure to observe both the challenges and positive changes that occur as a result of pressing pause. Perhaps you'll see things you don't need in your life. Maybe an excess will become more obvious as unhealthy habits show themselves. And you'll finally get some clear headspace to evaluate the way you want to lead and live. It may not be easy, but it will likely be an amazing return for a one-week fast!

SESSION WRAP-UP

Pressing pause helps us to see that life isn't just something we endure—it's meant to be lived to the fullest. As we engage in practices such as Sabbath rest and fasting, we discover our rhythm, which serves as a reminder, a way to remember, and a way to replenish. Pressing pause shows us there's something more—and this allows us to turn down the noise and seek some rest. Taken together, the four habits we have discussed in this study will help us turn down the noise, be fully present, and grow in our emotional health. This is not just a better way for us to live as individuals—it's also *how to lead in a world of distraction.*

PERSONAL STUDY

If you want to enhance your group study experience, consider doing any of the following activities on your own before the next meeting.

READ

Read chapter 9, "Pressing Pause," and chapter 10, "Master Control," in *How to Lead in a World of Distraction*. Write down some of your key takeaways from these chapters.

DO

Closely related to the idea of Sabbath is the *sabbatical*. While few of us are tenured professors who get three-month sabbaticals, we can all take a day or two on the weekend to practice pressing pause. This week set aside at least a few hours where you can slow down. Create space and let yourself breathe. Write down what this exercise revealed to you.

Watch the short video "Why We're Closed on Sundays," found at the Chick-fil-A website. What are some of the reasons given for why the restaurant shuts its doors on that day? What does this tell you about the importance of adopting a rhythm of pressing pause?

REFLECT

Read Exodus 20:8–11:

> Remember the Sabbath day by keeping it holy. Six days you shall labor and do all your work, but the seventh day is a sabbath to the LORD your God. On it you shall not do any work, neither you, nor your son or daughter, nor your male or female servant, nor your animals, nor any foreigner residing in your towns. For in six days the LORD made the heavens and the earth, the sea, and all that is in them, but he rested on the seventh day. Therefore the LORD blessed the Sabbath day and made it holy.

Reflect on these questions:

What command was God instructing his people to follow? Why did God take a day of rest after creation?

What does it mean to keep the Sabbath day holy? Why is it important to have a day to press pause and remember all that God has done for you?

Read Matthew 12:1–14:

At that time Jesus went through the grainfields on the Sabbath. His disciples were hungry and began to pick some heads of grain and eat them. When the Pharisees saw this, they said to him, "Look! Your disciples are doing what is unlawful on the Sabbath."

He answered, "Haven't you read what David did when he and his companions were hungry? He entered the house of God, and he and his companions ate the consecrated bread—which was not lawful for them to do, but only for the priests. Or haven't you read in the Law that the priests on Sabbath duty in the temple desecrate the Sabbath and yet are innocent? I tell you that something greater than the temple is here. If you had known what these words mean, 'I desire mercy, not sacrifice,' you would not have condemned the innocent. For the Son of Man is Lord of the Sabbath."

Going on from that place, he went into their synagogue, and a man with a shriveled hand was there. Looking for a reason to bring charges against Jesus, they asked him, "Is it lawful to heal on the Sabbath?"

He said to them, "If any of you has a sheep and it falls into a pit on the Sabbath, will you not take hold of it and lift it out? How much more valuable is a person than a sheep! Therefore it is lawful to do good on the Sabbath."

Then he said to the man, "Stretch out your hand." So he stretched it out and it was completely restored, just as sound as the other. But the Pharisees went out and plotted how they might kill Jesus.

Reflect on these questions:

What are some of the ways the Pharisees had taken the idea of the Sabbath to the extreme? What point do you think Jesus was making when he healed the man on the Sabbath?

What does this say about the real purpose of the Sabbath?

APPLY

Pressing pause and choosing to fast for a specific season allows you to remember what is most important. What is something important you've lost sight of by running nonstop? Are you willing to slow down to regain your focus?

ABOUT
THE AUTHOR

Clay Scroggins is the lead pastor of Buckhead Church, one of the largest campuses of North Point Ministries, where he provides visionary and directional leadership for the church's staff and attendees. Starting out as a facilities intern (aka vice president of nothing), he has worked his way through several organizational levels at North Point Ministries. Clay holds a degree in industrial engineering from Georgia Tech as well as a master's degree and a doctorate with an emphasis in online church from Dallas Theological Seminary. He is the author of *How to Lead When You're Not in Charge* and lives in Atlanta with his wife, Jenny, and their five children.

Also available from Clay Scroggins

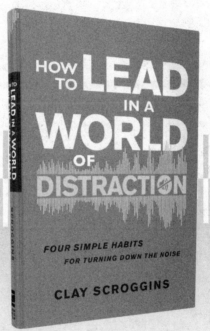

How to Lead When You're Not in Charge

Leveraging Influence When You Lack Authority

Clay Scroggins

"This book will be one of the most, if not the most, pivotal leadership books you'll ever read." –Andy Stanley

"If you're ready to lead right where you are, this book can show you how to start." –Dave Ramsey

"Read this book! The marketplace is full of many helpful leadership messages, but this one is a standout." –Louie Giglio

One of the greatest myths of leadership is that you must be in charge in order to lead. Great leaders don't buy it. Great leaders lead with or without the authority and learn to unleash their influence wherever they are.

With practical wisdom and humor, Clay Scroggins will help you nurture your vision and cultivate influence, even when you lack authority in your organization. And he will free you to become the great leader you want to be so you can make a difference right where you are. Even when you're not in charge.

Available in stores and online!

How to Lead When You're Not in Charge Study Guide with DVD

Leveraging Influence When You Lack Authority

Clay Scroggins

One of the greatest myths of leadership is that you must be in charge in order to lead. Great leaders don't buy it. Great leaders lead with or without the authority and learn to unleash their influence wherever they are.

With practical wisdom and humor, author and pastor Clay Scroggins will help you nurture your vision and cultivate influence, even when you lack authority in your organization. And he will free you to become the great leader you want to be so you can make a difference right where you are. Even when you're not in charge.

In this six-session video study, Clay explains what is needed to be a great leader—even when you answer to someone else.

Sessions include:

1. The Oddity of Leadership
2. Lead Yourself
3. Choose Positivity
4. Think Critically
5. Reject Passivity
6. Challenging Up

This pack contains one study guide and one DVD.

Available in stores and online!